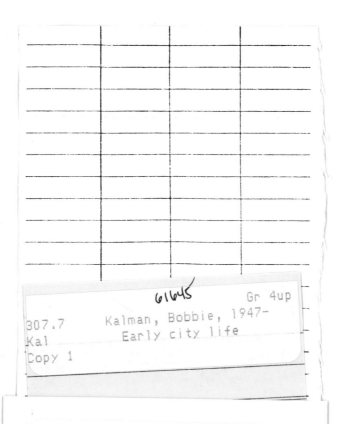

Early City Life

Bobbie Kalman

The Early Settler Life Series

Toronto
New York

Crabtree Publishing Company

To Alan, Anne, John, Ann, and David

A special thanks to the following people without whose help this book would not have been possible:

Senior editor: *Lise Gunby*
Researcher: *Maria Protz*
Assistant editors: *Susan Hughes*
Mary Ann Horgan
Diane Taylor
Carla Williams
Freelance editor: *Dan Liebman*
Design and mechanicals: *Nancy Cook*
Artwork pages 28 and 29: *Gary Pearson*
Photographers: *Sarah Peters*
Stephen Mangione
Donna Acheson
Picture researchers: *Noel Rutland*
Linda Kudo
Librarians: *Margaret Crawford Maloney*
Dana Tenny
Jill Shefrin
Stanley Triggs

A thank you to Arnie Krause for keeping us on schedule

Cataloging in Publication Data

Kalman, Bobbie, 1947 -
  Early City Life

(Early settler life series)
Includes index.
ISBN   0-86505-029-5 hardcover
ISBN   0-86505-028-7 softcover

1. City and town life - History.
I. Title.   II. Series.

HT119.K334 1983   307.7'6'0903

102 Torbrick Avenue
Toronto M4J 4Z5

350 Fifth Avenue
Suite 3308
New York, N.Y. 10001

Contents

This old photograph shows us some of the reasons why this city grew. It is near water. Ships from other ports can dock here, bringing supplies. The railway connects the city to other cities and towns.

Why did cities grow?

Why did some early settlements grow into cities while others did not? The answer is not simple. There are many reasons why a city develops. Some of the important reasons are given below. Can you think of other reasons? What makes cities grow today?

Geographic location

One of the major reasons that cities grew was geographic location. Cities grew along the east coast first because ships from Europe docked there, bringing new supplies. Being near water assured the settlers of goods and services, which made their lives easier. In the early days it was nearly impossible to travel on land. There were no roads. There was only forest. For many years water routes were the only practical way to transport goods and passengers.

Important services

The building of a gristmill or sawmill was a joyous occasion for the settlers. Mills made grinding grain and preparing lumber faster

and simpler. They attracted new settlers. Merchants built stores and homes near these mills. Towns began to grow. Some of these towns expanded into small cities.

Protection

In some parts of the country, military forts offered protection to the settlers who lived near them. The fort itself was a small community. Inside its walls were blacksmiths, harness makers, and wheelwrights. Settlers traded and visited with the military families who lived inside the fort. Some of the soldiers were educated people who offered companionship and entertainment to the sometimes lonely settlers. The military knew the latest news and kept the settlers up-to-date on world developments.

Overland connections

As villages grew, roadways were cleared to connect them. Overland transportation became possible. Better roads were built. People were able to travel in stagecoaches.

Towns grew into cities, and the new cities did not stop growing. Cities attracted more residents than villages or towns did. Cities offered work, education, and an opportunity for people to practice the religion of their choice.

Inns were constructed to house travelers and to feed and water their horses. More settlers were attracted to towns served by coach routes. These towns quickly increased in size.

New connections by railroad

Railways caused many towns to grow so fast that they seemed to turn into cities overnight. The railroads made it possible to move large numbers of people and large amounts of goods overland. Towns that were far from water transportation became easy to reach.

Discovery of raw materials

Minerals were discovered and mined in the mountains. Coal and iron ore mines were opened. Steel mills were built. The search for gold took many people west. Factories were built. People came to work in the factories. Cities grew where there were many people.

The prospect of different jobs

People moved to different parts of the country to work at paid jobs. Girls and boys who grew up on farms began to leave home to go to the cities. Sometimes the family farm could not support them. Sometimes they wanted adventure and the companionship of other young people.

Bigger industries, bigger cities

The cities were attractive to new settlers from other countries. Factory owners encouraged them to come and work. Many emigrants were used to living in cities. They wanted the comforts of city life. Their occupations suited the city. Some were trained to work in factories and textile mills. Some emigrants were lawyers and doctors. Others were builders, storekeepers, seamstresses, servants, teachers, preachers, and carpenters.

What is a city?

Look at this drawing of an early city. A city is a large community which includes many smaller communities. A community is a group of people living in the same area and sharing goods, services, and the same government. What made a city grow and operate? What does a city need? People, of

course! Without plenty of people there would be no city. What else does a city need? Try to guess!
Twelve important things that a city needs are shown on the next two pages. How many of them
did you guess? How many of them are related to the drawing of this city?

Cities need...

People Cities need people. The bigger a city grows, the more new people it attracts.

Leadership People need a government to carry out their wishes.

Protection There are many dangers in a city. People need to be protected from these dangers.

Services Roads need to be built, repaired, and cleaned. Traffic must be controlled.

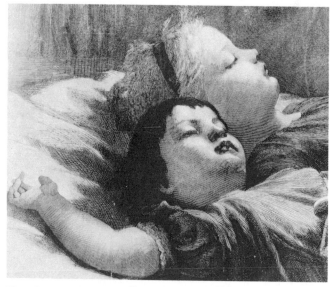

Food and Shelter People need food. They also need protection from the weather.

Education Schools are built in which to educate the city's young people.

Culture People with many different traditions and talents create the cultural life of the city.

Transportation The city provides public coaches and streetcars for those who do not own wagons.

Communication Letters and newspapers keep the city settlers in touch with new events.

Occupations The city offers many different opportunities for employment.

Business and commerce New businesses and shops provide more jobs and money for the city.

Leisure People need time to relax. City dwellers enjoy interesting pastimes.

Cary met Sue in an interesting way. He was hard at work and happened to glance at the building next door. There she was, hard at work too! Cary started to work in the city as a mason. He invested his money wisely and soon made a small fortune in the real-estate business.

Moving into the city

What do all cities have in common? People! All kinds of people flocked to the early city. People left farming communities to find jobs in the exciting new city. Immigrants were attracted to the opportunities offered by the city.

Let Mr. Crookshank and Mr. Salvos tell you their reasons for moving to the city:

My name is Cary Crookshank. My parents came to this country and bought a farm. My brothers and sisters grew up loving the farm life. I was happier to be sent to school in the city.

*I learned to be a **mason.** I was hired by a private company. I liked my work. I met Sue when I was laying bricks for a building. High above the roofs of the city, we fell in love.*

When my Pa died, he left me enough money to set myself up in business. He expected me to buy a brickworks but I took the notion to look around a bit. One day I heard that a whole block of tenements was on fire. The block was burned to the ground by nightfall. The landlords did not want to be bothered with building again, so I bought the land from them. Within a year, a new warehouse was needed at the docks, so I built one on my land. When I sold the building, Sue and I got married and began to plan for the future.

Living off the land

Sue and I started thinking about land. The city was growing, and we knew that land was cheap now but would soon be expensive. We bought land in the city at the low prices and held onto it. When the prices rose, we sold the land and made a profit. I continued my masonry work, but we continued buying and selling land. We bought property outside the borders of the city. When the city grew, the bordering land became valuable. It wasn't hard to sell it for three times as much as we had paid for it.

*After ten years of buying and selling, my wife and I established our own **real-estate** company. With people working for me, we can afford to relax a little more. We are quite wealthy now. We are like my Ma and Pa. We owe our wealth to the land. We use the land in a different way than my parents did. We built our life on it, buying and selling.*

Building a better life

Mr. Salvos came to this country as a young man. He decided to live and work in the early city. This is his story.

I am from Italy. I was born on the bed my father built and was rocked in the cradle his hands carved. My father was the best furniture maker in our town. I was the youngest of seven boys, and every one of us grew up to be a wood-worker. I guess we just cannot do without the smell of sawdust!

There was not enough work for all of us in the one town. All my brothers moved to other towns in the country but I, young and a dreamer, had heard of the land of oppor-tunity. I set sail for the New World!

Good luck and hard work

After a long journey, the ship docked at the harbor in this city. I was a stranger in a foreign country, and it was good to me. When I learned that there were only a few furniture makers in the city, I could not believe my luck. I started my business as soon as I could, bringing in wood from the forests outside of the city and beginning with only simple and practical kinds of furniture. I would build a chair. The next day it would be sold. I would build a table. That afternoon it would be sold!

If I do say so myself, the other furniture makers in the city were not experts at their craft. People were happy to pay whatever price I asked for my finely-crafted wares. Soon I was making money. I could send some back to my parents and even afford to hire some apprentices for my shop. Oh, I was fortunate to come to this country! The city was growing and growing. Although other furniture makers arrived, there was enough demand for our products to keep us all busy. My apprentices had good hands. Soon I could let them build the basic furniture, and I was free to make the fancy pieces which I love so much!

My business is still doing well. A desire to take a chance, luck, hard work, and skill are the reasons behind my success story. Oh yes, I am a happy man!

*City planners are debating whether or not to build a second bridge across the river that divides the city. The planner believes that the city cannot afford a new bridge unless the residents pay more taxes. The angry mayor has his hands on his hips. He believes that a second bridge must be built because the traffic is terrible on the first bridge. The city can charge a **toll** to pay for the bridge.*

*Mr. Whipple is not a popular **candidate**! He made a speech about raising taxes to pay for a bigger City Hall. The voters are making it very clear that they do not like the idea.*

Organizing the city

The city grew quickly as stores and businesses opened. New people arrived every day, looking for jobs and homes. Houses and tenements sprang up to provide shelter for the new residents. As cities became busier, they became more complicated. They needed to be organized. Factories had to be built far from the streets where people lived. Hospitals and schools had to be built in convenient locations. Land had to be set aside for train stations and shipping docks. The residents needed roads and public transportation. They needed lights for their streets. They needed water. They needed a sanitation system to keep the city clean.

Organizing a city was hard work. The mayor was boss. He had a planning committee to help him take care of the city. The committee met at City Hall. City Hall was a large, handsome building in the center of the city. Residents of the city were elected to this **municipal** government. City planners had important jobs and were important people in the city. During elections, they **campaigned** to convince people to vote for them. They made speeches about why they were the best candidates for the job.

The City Hall was usually the grandest building in the city. Can you guess where it is in this picture? The church is the building with the steeple. City churches were also elaborate. A farmer has parked his oxen and wagon near the City Hall. He is inside, offering to sell his land to the city. The city needs more land. The farmer can get a good price for his farm and buy cheaper land farther away.

Taxes for services

Where would the city government get the money needed to pay for buildings, transportation, sanitation, and other city services? The money was raised through taxation. City residents paid for the city services by giving money to the government. People who owned houses or businesses paid taxes. People who rented places to live and did not own businesses were not taxed by the city.

How many windows do you have in your home? This question may seem silly, but it was serious to the early city residents. One method of taxing property was to tax windows. Windows were expensive. People with more windows in their homes or buildings paid more taxes.

Municipal governments collected **direct taxes** as well as property taxes. A direct tax was collected each time a service was used. A **toll**, for example, was a direct tax. When an expensive road or bridge was built, the city paid for it by charging a fee each time people used it. Governments still use tolls to help pay the cost of bridges. Perhaps you have crossed a toll bridge.

The skyline of growing cities changed every day. These men are building a huge bridge. The bridge will allow the city to expand. Factories will be built across the river.

13

Fires spread so quickly that often the only hope was the bravery of the firemen. This baby was caught in a room surrounded by flames. There was no way for his parents to save him. Firemen risked burning to death by going to the rescue through the window.

Firemen worked all night with their fire hoses to stop the blaze in this downtown building. It is so cold outside that the water used to douse the fire has frozen into icicles.

Fire!

Fire was a terrible hazard in the early cities. Firefighters had important, dangerous, and difficult jobs. They did not have the fire-fighting system that we have today. There were no fire hydrants. The fire brigade had to take water from the water pumps shared by all the people who lived on a street. It was hard to pump water fast enough to stop the flames. In the early days, there were not even fire hoses. The water was thrown on the flames. Firefighters formed long lines from the pumps to the blaze and passed water buckets from person to person. This line of firefighters was called a "bucket brigade."

Fires in the cities spread so quickly that a small blaze could easily become a disaster. Whole neighborhoods could be destroyed. Houses and other buildings stood so close together that the flames leapt from one building to the next. Some city fires raged for days. The fire brigade worked without sleep, trying to control the blaze and to prevent further damage.

Police officers protected people from criminals. They also helped people in trouble. Beth was separated from her parents on a visit to the crowded docks.

A prisoner is allowed to see a visitor, who reads the newspaper to him. Prisons were built in the early cities to protect innocent citizens against crime.

Public protection

In many new towns there were no police because there were few criminals. A town often had a couple of troublemakers, but there was a watchman to see that they did not cause much harm. The watchman strolled up and down the streets at night to make sure the neighborhood was safe and sound. Residents could hear him shout regularly "All's well!" The watchman watched. He also was a watch! He shouted out the correct time as he patrolled the streets.

As towns grew into cities, problems and crime increased. Police officers were hired to protect the public. They had "beats" or neighborhoods which they guarded. Offenders were arrested. If they were convicted in court, they were often sent to prison.

City prisons were miserable places. In some prisons, criminals wore iron collars and chains. They were beaten and whipped. Today we try to help criminals improve their lives. In the early days, criminals were simply punished.

As cities grew, citizens needed more people to protect them. Traffic controllers, security guards, and dogcatchers were hired by City Hall. Lifeguards prevented drowning accidents.

15

These pedestrians are curious. Few of them have seen a road being paved. Most streets were made of cobblestones or boards. Can you see the cobblestones in this picture? Soon they will be covered with pavement. Paving is hard work. The laborers have only a few machines to help them.

How can you tell this is a picture of an early city? Look at the road. Does it give you a clue? It is made of boards.

Street services

One of the first **services** that cities provided for their residents was the building of roads. The city government collected taxes to pay for road building, cleaning, and repairing.

The first streets were made of planks of wood or **cobblestones**. In later years, city streets were paved. To save money, the city often paved only the middle of the roads, where the carriages traveled. The sidewalks and gutters were added later to make traveling on the streets cleaner and easier.

In the winter, huge snowdrifts often blocked roads. Workers were hired to shovel the streets to make way for the carriages and streetcars. Sidewalks were also cleared for people who enjoyed winter walks. During the dusty summer, cleaners were employed to wash the streets. They drove horse-drawn carts carrying sprinklers. The sprinkler was a barrel of water with many holes around the bottom. Water flowed out of these holes and onto the dirty street. An army of sweepers worked daily to keep city streets clean. This was not an easy job. No matter how hard the sweepers worked, more garbage always replaced yesterday's dirt.

Children loved to see the street washer coming on a hot, sunny day. They followed his sprinkler along the street, dancing under its spray. How good it felt to clean your hot feet! What else is there in the picture that shows you it is a hot, sunny day?

Snow, snow, and more snow! There was nothing to do but pile it up! Hiring people to shovel snow from roads and public walkways was one of the jobs of the city government.

The street sweepers gather in the morning for roll call. They prefer their jobs to factory work. At least they are outside and can sometimes stop for a chat with pedestrians.

17

Finding shelter

*Shelter is a basic human need. Some people in the city lived in luxurious homes or apartments. Others occupied uncomfortable tenements or shacks. Sometimes old and sick people were forced to seek shelter in buildings such as churches and hospitals. This picture shows the contrast between the dwellings for the poor and the dwellings for people with money. The poor people who lived in the shacks were called **squatters**. They did not own land and could not afford to rent shelter. They simply built their **shanty town** on property owned by the city.*

This home is owned by a wealthy city lawyer. Each member of the family has a bedroom. A beautiful garden surrounds the house. Many city dwellers could not afford the luxury of a beautiful home and garden.

Some people had no homes. These children are orphans. They must find warmth near a steam vent. There are not enough orphanages for all of the homeless children. The people walking by are going to comfortable homes.

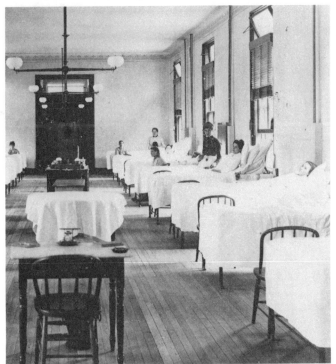

Some sick people had diseases that could not be cured. There were a few charity hospitals where these people could live. Often the patients spent their lives in hospitals. These early hospitals were nothing more than a shelter for poor people who were ill. They offered little medical care.

In the country, people lived in **extended** families. Grandparents and other relatives lived in the same house as the children and their parents. **Nuclear** families were more common in the city. Only children and parents lived together. Sometimes older people were left homeless. These senior citizens found shelter and food in a home provided by their local church.

Comfortable homes

The well-to-do settlers lived in beautiful homes with stables and gardens. This old house is located near the middle of the city. It has four stories, including a cellar. It contains many rooms: bedrooms, workrooms, servants' quarters, living rooms, a parlor, and two kitchens. Many houses, such as this one, did not have a bathroom. Each house had a **privy**, or outhouse, in the back yard. There is no number on the front door of this house. People used **landmarks** instead of addresses. If you were to ask directions to a house, a neighbor would tell you, for example, to turn left at the tall oak tree and then turn right after passing a white gate.

Many of the city settlers had a small garden patch behind their homes. They grew flowers, herbs, vegetables, and fruit there. Some of the city dwellers even kept animals, such as chickens, goats, and pigs. One could be sure of having fresh food by raising or growing it right at home. There was a bit of the old farming spirit still left in many city dwellers.

Fancy homes often had two kitchens, a pantry, and an ice house in which food was kept cold. One kitchen was used in the winter. The second was a summer kitchen. Servants cooked the meals. The meals were carried to the dining room in a **dumbwaiter,** which was like a small elevator. Early kitchens had fireplaces. Later, stoves were built into the old fireplaces.

The parlor was a special room. It was reserved as a place to entertain guests and for special occasions. Father plays the piano for the family. Most of the other family members also know how to play the piano. Music was important, and there were no radios or stereos. The piano was a family treasure.

Doing the family laundry was a huge chore. Water had to be carried from the pump and then heated in the fireplace or on the stove.

The water supply

Can you imagine not being able to turn on a faucet and have hot and cold running water? The early city dwellers did not even know what a faucet was! A few families had wells with pumps, but in most neighborhoods people had to share the use of a common pump. This meant that the pump was always busy. Servants went to the pumps early in the morning to fill buckets with water. People drank water right at the pumps from ladles provided for public use. They did not know that they were catching other people's germs. In later years a city water-pipe system was installed, but people were suspicious of it. They thought that water from wells was better than water that ran through the pipes. Many people bought their drinking water from water vendors who sold it by the jug or bottle.

Sewage

The early city sewage system was not like the one used today. At first, sewers were built to carry away water that flooded in the spring. Later, sewers were connected to the houses. City dwellers were then able to pump the contents of their **cesspools** into the sewers. Garbage and wastes were thrown into the cesspools, which were dug outside the house. The sewage was drained out through the sewers and into a river nearby. The wastes were not filtered. The settlers did not know about germs, so they did not realize how this raw sewage could make them ill. In poor areas, the sewage was dumped right into the major river flowing through the city. Many diseases were caused by contaminated river water and filthy water-supply systems.

Bathing

It is hard to imagine how the settlers could have put up with such poor conditions. Things were not much better inside. Most early homes did not have bathrooms. People did not like to bathe because they thought it was not healthy. They feared they would develop pneumonia if they bathed too often. When people did have a bath, they filled tin tubs with water, which they heated on the stove. The whole family then took turns bathing in the same water.

As the population increased, people realized that personal hygiene and city sanitation must be improved. People were dying from cholera, a disease that spread because garbage and human waste were everywhere. The city began to solve the problems caused by the lack of hygiene. Sewage systems were improved. Public bathhouses were built to encourage people to bathe. People started to feel good about being clean.

Central heating appeared in later days. It made city homes warmer and cosier throughout. Father puts more coal into the cellar furnace. Mother takes an armful of wood up to the kitchen stove, which is now used only for cooking and baking.

Light and heat

Fireplaces, candles, and oil lamps provided light for the early city homes. Candles were made of **tallow,** or melted-down fat. Some candles were also made of bayberries and beeswax, but these were very expensive. Oil lamps were used in the homes of the rich. Some families used lard as fuel because it was cheaper than oil.

The area around the kitchen fireplace was the most popular spot in the early city home. There was usually one huge fireplace in the kitchen. The fire was kept burning night and day. There were also fireplaces in the bedrooms, which kept the family warm while they slept. In later days, stoves replaced fireplaces. The heat from stoves stayed in the room and did not go up the chimney, as it did with the fireplace.

At first the fireplace provided both light and heat for the settlers. Families huddled around its flames each evening to read, sew, tell stories, or just enjoy the warmth of the fire.

23

This family has nothing to eat or drink except soup and coffee. The landlord has come to collect the rent, but the family has no money to give him. Bessie is afraid and hides behind her mother. The landlord feels sorry for the family and will give them another week before they must pay.

This family has just been turned out of their tenement apartment because they could not pay the rent. Father broke his arm and cannot work. He and Mother wonder where they and their young children will live.

Tenement life

Many immigrants came to this country hoping to buy land. Often it was impossible for them to own property in their native countries. In some countries, many people simply had no hope of ever earning enough money to buy land. In this country, anyone who earned enough money could buy land. Unfortunately, property was often expensive in the cities. Some immigrants found that they could not afford to buy land in the city. They were forced to rent space in **tenement** buildings at high costs.

Danger at Home

Many tenements were miserable places to live. Landlords were unkind to the tenants and frequently raised the rent. Rats, mice, and insects occupied the crowded tenements. Although these buildings had fire escapes, the fire routes were often cluttered with the laundry or the other belongings of the tenants. Few precautions against fire were taken. These buildings were often firetraps.

Yesterday's slums

The tenement buildings were badly constructed. They had poor ventilation and lighting. The buildings could be sizzling hot in the summer and freezing cold in the winter. Poor drainage and sewer systems sent bad odors through these buildings. It was usually impossible for tenants to cook meals because few tenement apartments had kitchens. There were no bathrooms either. Public bathrooms were sometimes many blocks from a tenement building.

Many people could not even rent an apartment in one of the tenement buildings. Either they did not have enough money or there was no space available. Some of these people lived in the cellars of tenement buildings. Cellars were cheap and another person could always be squeezed in. The tenants kept pigs, chickens, and sometimes even horses and cattle in the cellar. They survived on the milk and eggs from the animals or sold the produce to others.

Not all of the poor people lived in downtown tenement buildings. Many squatters lived in "shanty towns" or slums on the outskirts of the city. The squatter's home was usually no larger than two rooms. The shanties were built of odds and ends. Could you build a house of wood, corncobs, and stones? A **daubing** was a common event in the shack town. When a newlywed couple needed a home, friends of the bride and groom built them a shanty on their wedding day. After the new shanty was patched together, the day ended with food and dancing.

These shacks did not stand upright for long. Too much money was required to keep them in good repair. One bad storm could ruin a squatter home. At least the shanties were warm and dry for as long as they lasted. Often they were more comfortable than the tenements downtown. As the city expanded, small modern bungalows gradually replaced the shack towns.

George would have been happy to live in a tenement. Since his parents have died, he has had no home at all. He wanders the streets looking for odd jobs and places to sleep. There were few orphanages in those days.

Soup kitchens were run by the churches. Poor people who could not afford to buy food lined up for a hot meal. A bowl of soup was worth a wait in the cold. In this picture, you can see the volunteers preparing the soup. A poor family walks to the church building to wait for seats. The people are so hungry that they can hardly wait to be served.

Churches were involved in caring for the sick. Many hospitals and nursing orders were established by different religious groups. The government provided very little medical care.

Church and charity

There were many types of people and many religious faiths in the city. People of all religions shared a concern for the unfortunate. One of the most important beliefs was to "Love thy neighbor." Wealthy people sometimes helped the poor by giving money to the church. Donations were the only funds available to poor people because governments did not spend tax money on programs for the needy. The donations from kind and thoughtful people saved many lives.

Donations found their way to the poor in different ways. Soup kitchens were opened by the churches. They helped the poor by giving them a good, hot meal. It was worth waiting in line for a hot meal, especially in the chilly winter. Secondhand clothes were given to the needy. Concerned people formed groups for the purpose of visiting the sick and the poor.

Educational opportunities

City schools provided a better education for children than many of the one-room country schools. Here, children of the same age learned together. When the children graduated from elementary school, they had more choices. They could go to high school, trade school, or to colleges, where they could train to be doctors, lawyers, and teachers.

These boys are taking a woodworking course in a city trade school. They will have a better chance in the future because of their special education. Later, they can open their own shops or become managers in large factories.

Melissa writes a letter for her mother. Her mother never learned to read or write. Melissa is lucky because she will have a chance to get a good education in the city.

27

The many fa

The little girl in the picture is lost. The boys cannot understand her language but they offer their help and friendship. They too were once new to this country. City people came from all walks of life, from every country in the world. In the early days, almost everyone was an immigrant. One of the most exciting parts of city life was meeting people from other cultures. People from many countries brought with them exciting ways of life. Exotic foods, colorful dress, and lively music were just a few of the

daily enjoyments shared by city residents.
Immigrants flooded the city with gifts of the
arts. Painters, musicians, writers, and inventors made valuable contributions. As time
passed, more and more immigrants came to live
in the cities. Even today, there are many new-
comers. The city is a world of many cultures.
People contribute their unique ways of life and
discover other ways of living. To appreciate
the customs and ideas of other people is one of
life's biggest joys.

The art gallery has a new sculpture. Everyone is eager to see it. People of all ages enjoy visiting the gallery. Art galleries collected famous works of art from all over the world. City residents had the chance to share the beauty of famous paintings and sculptures.

Can you guess what these women are doing? They are acting in a pantomime. They must tell a story with their movements because they are not allowed to speak. Can you make up a story to match their body language? There were always pantomimes and other kinds of plays to see at the theater.

Today, turtles are becoming scarce. They are now a protected species. Many countries have made it illegal to import products made from turtles. In the early days, turtle soup was a popular item on restaurant menus. City restaurants were a delight to those who enjoyed sampling new foods. People could try interesting recipes from many different lands.

Love that city life!

Dear Mother,

John and I will celebrate our first wedding anniversary next week. It is hard to realize that we have lived in the city for a whole year. I recall my first few months here, when I could not believe that I would ever be happy again. How I hated all the noise! I was terrified of stepping outside the house. City people seemed to dash about, not even bothering to look where they were going. I thought that I would be trampled to death crossing the streets!

Now memories of those early months make me chuckle. Oh, the city is as noisy and crowded as ever, the air is still foul, but now I love it! I've discovered that the city's good points outweigh its faults. Ever since John's accounting business has started to do well, we have been able to enjoy the finer parts of city life. If you could only try some of the marvelous city restaurants. John and

I go to a different spot each week. So far we've eaten German, French, Italian, and Far Eastern food. Immigrants from many lands have brought such interesting recipes.

John and I have gone to the theater several times. The costumes are magnificent. I especially love the opera. The singers leave me breathless. Last week, we went to view an exhibit of paintings from England. There is so much entertainment in our city! There is an amusement park and a zoo. While walking down the street, one can hear the merry organ grinder as he plays his songs on the corner. The children love to dance and spin to his tunes.

This is a strange party! It is a masquerade ball. Everyone is dressed in a costume, and it is not Halloween. Masquerade balls gave city residents a chance to meet friends and use their imaginations. Which costume do you like best?

Yacht races were popular events on weekends in the city. People dressed up and went to the harbor. On the pier, people are watching the race through binoculars and small telescopes. Some people are not even watching the race. They are simply enjoying one another's company.

Never a dull moment

I miss the tranquility of the country at times. Every now and then I long for the sight of swallows swooping in the barnyard and grain blowing in the fields. Still, I must confess I have grown to love the constant murmur of the city. John and I meet so many interesting people here. There is never a dull moment.

I think it would be wonderful if you came to visit us. There is such a variety of shops. There is one store in particular, Mother, which carries nothing but imported European dresses. They are so fine! If you come to visit, John promises to have one fitted for you. Please bring my dear brother and sister as well. I am sure that Rosalie would love the theater and masquerades. Both she and Francis would enjoy going to some of the sporting events. John and I love the weekend boat races at the harbor.

I miss you all. It would make me very happy to have you come and stay with us for a while. I want so much to show you what city life is all about.

Your loving daughter,

Alexandra

Have you ever been to the opera? The audience is waiting for the curtain to rise. The orchestra is warming up. Soon the lights will go down and the beautiful sounds and sights will begin.

Why might you think that this is a very early city? Perhaps you would point out the gas lamps and the horse-drawn taxis. This city, however, has electricity. What clues show that electricity has been discovered?

What a mob! At rush hour in the city, bicycles were useless. People had to carry them to get through the crowd! Trolleys were the fastest, newest method of transportation, but these electric streetcars sometimes derailed!

"If you care about your child and your purse, Miss, don't ride on this crowded trolley!" the conductor said to the lady. This picture appeared in an old newspaper to show people the dangers of public transportation. The crowds in the trolleys made it easy for criminals to do their dirty work.

Taxis and trolleys

There were many ways for residents to travel in the city. Wealthy people could afford private transportation. They had their own coaches and teams of horses. Other people hired taxis. Taxis were small coaches hitched to one horse. The driver sat on top of the coach. When people wanted a ride, they waved to flag him down. In the winter, people used sleighs as taxis.

The city also offered public transportation. Public buses stopped along the streets to pick up passengers. These "buses" were large coaches pulled by four or more horses. Later, streetcars drawn by horses were used. Some people called them **trolleys.** Trolleys ran on steel rails which were built into the paved streets. Trolleys were a popular kind of transportation because they were cheaper than taxis. They were often quite uncomfortable. In the winter, they were like moving ice boxes! In the summer, the crowded trolleys were hotter than steam cookers! Sometimes streetcars were so crowded that people had to hold on to the outside of a moving trolley. This certainly was a dangerous way to get across town!

Traffic troubles

Pickpockets and petty thieves loved to ride the crowded trolleys. They could pick a pocket and jump off. Robbing travelers was an easy way to make a dishonest day's wages!

Driving in the city was never fun. Traffic moved slowly because there were no traffic lights. The confusion and noise caused serious accidents. In the winter, trolleys flew off the track and got stuck in high snow drifts.

Traffic jams caused serious problems for everyone. People who decided to walk had difficulties. Pedestrians were risking their lives when they tried to cross the streets during rush hour!

City traffic was noisy and dirty as well as dangerous. After the train was invented, the situation became even worse. Trains caused more accidents, more noise, and more air pollution.

Josephine mails a letter to her husband. He has gone back to visit his sick father. Josephine could not go with him because the baby is too young for a long journey. Letters were the only way for people to communicate across long distances.

Keeping in touch

In the country, the owner of the general store usually took care of mail for the community. In the early city, the post office was in a large building. There were no letter carriers walking from house to house. There were no mailboxes or postage stamps. Envelopes had not been invented. How was a letter mailed?

Mary Ann's cousin lives in a distant city. Mary Ann wants to invite Alison to visit. She must write a letter. There is no such thing as a telephone! Mary Ann writes her letter on a sturdy piece of paper. She carefully folds the paper, with the blank side of the

paper facing out. Then she begins to seal her letter. She drops a little melted wax where the folded pages meet. She takes the family **seal** and presses it into the wax. Alison will know as soon as she sees the letter that it comes from Mary Ann's home. If the seal is broken, Alison will know that someone else has read her letter!

Mary Ann walks to the post office to mail her letter. She does not have to pay to send it. When Alison receives the letter, she must pay. Mary Ann knows, however, that she will have to pay to find out whether Alison accepts her invitation!

Dawn breaks in the city. The newsboys scramble to get bundles of newspapers. They must hurry to their favorite street corners, where they will sell the papers to the pedestrians hurrying by. Newsboys were often street waifs who needed their jobs in order to survive.

What's news?

Something exciting was always happening in the city. In the country, people met at the general store to exchange news. In the city, people read the daily and weekly newspapers. Reporters roamed the streets looking for "all the news that's fit to print." The newspaper offices were always busy with reporters and editors clattering away at typewriters and shouting at the copy boy who ran errands for them. The news had to be new, and everyone in the office was rushing to meet deadlines.

Ricky is a newsboy. Someday he wants to be a reporter. He hopes that he will be able to go to school, but now he must earn his living selling newspapers. He is an orphan. The newspaper provides him with a small amount of money for food and shelter. Every morning he is up at dawn to collect bundles of newspapers. He sells the papers on the street corners. "Read all about it," he shouts to the people hurrying to work.

Ricky likes to read the newspaper when his work is done. He does not read very well, but can understand most of the words. The newspaper contains so much information. There are news stories, weather reports, articles about interesting people, and even short stories, jokes, and cartoons. Every day the editors write their opinions about situations or events in **editorials.** Stores advertise their bargains. The newspaper is truly the guide to city life.

"Read all about it! Read all about it!"

Mr. Peabody is reading over a land deed. His client wants to sell his property. Mr. Peabody is checking to make sure that the agreement between his client and the buyer is ready to be signed and sealed.

Dr. Rogers listens to Tom describe his symptoms. In the country, doctors often made house calls. In the city, they opened their own offices.

The professionals

Many experts in different professions were needed in the growing city. **Professionals** were people who were skilled in certain jobs. Most professionals studied at colleges and universities to learn their skills. Professionals such as doctors, lawyers, architects, and engineers served the special needs of the city and its people.

Many of the diseases and illnesses that we have treatments and cures for today were killers in the past. Many doctors and nurses worked directly with patients. Others worked as researchers in hospitals and laboratories. These medical scientists discovered many of the medicines that save lives today.

Lawyers served people who disagreed about who was right and who was wrong. Disputes about property, tenancy, working conditions, and other business matters were solved in **civil** courts. Lawyers also defended or prosecuted people charged with crimes. These trials were held in **criminal** courts. Lawyers and judges worked hard to support fair and just laws.

These clerks work in the office of a large company. They are called "white-collar" workers. You can see why. When the company managers need information, the clerks always have it at their fingertips.

Making the city work

Many professions cooperated to plan and construct the city. Architects and engineers designed and planned beautiful buildings. Engineers also planned roads, sidewalks, water systems, and street lighting. Land surveyors examined and marked off the sites where new buildings would be constructed, and where sewers and other services would be located.

Professionals were called "white-collar" workers because of the way they dressed for work. Men worked in white shirts, ties, and suits. People whose jobs included physical labor were called "blue-collar" workers. Construction workers and factory workers wore practical, everyday clothes when they were on the job. They were paid according to how many hours they worked. They earned **wages**. White-collar workers earned **salaries**. They were paid a certain amount of money each week.

Accountants and clerks

Some white-collar workers were not considered to be professionals. They did not have to attend school for as long as doctors and lawyers did. They worked in offices.

Accountants worked for businesses and the government. They kept track of the money made and spent by businesses. They tried to balance the budgets of the government.

Clerks did a variety of tasks. Office clerks took care of the mail and letter writing. They organized the office records and files. **Retail** clerks worked in stores to help the customers. They answered questions about store merchandise, filled the orders for their customers, and helped them to carry packages. Many offices and stores also had errand boys to do odd jobs. They sharpened pencils, filled inkwells, and delivered messages.

Working in the factories

You can see from this picture how "lunch buckets" and "lunch pails" got their names. These people are walking to work. Men, women, and children all work at the factories near the harbor. People came from all over this country and from many other countries to get jobs in the cities.

This is one of the first canning factories with machines and an **assembly line.** One by one these cans are being sealed. The man is operating the machine. After the machine fills and seals the cans, it pastes on the labels and puts the cans in boxes, ready to be sent to the store.

Young women moved to the cities to find jobs. They worked long hours for low wages. Many of them worked in the garment industry. These workers are sewing clothes which will be sold in department stores. The workers are paid according to how many items they finish each day.

Young children worked 12 to 16 hours a day. These children labor in a brickyard. They are carrying clay to the kilns where it will be baked into bricks. Finally, laws were passed to prevent children from working at these terrible jobs.

*These women and children are taking work home. They are **pieceworkers**. Pieceworkers were paid for each piece of work they finished. The workers earned very little money, but their employers made large profits from their work.*

41

Maurice is the neighborhood milkman. He makes his rounds early each morning. His customers bring empty milk jugs to the wagon, where Maurice fills the jugs with fresh milk. Maurice is waiting for Mrs. Owens to come to collect her day's supply of milk.

The ice-cream vendors always rang the bells on their carts as they came down the street. When children heard them coming they rushed outside with their coins to buy a cold treat.

This monger is selling animals for people to take home for dinner. One woman wants to buy the rabbit. She is not hungry. She wants a pet!

Would anyone like to buy some wood? Wood vendors often got cold as they worked cutting kindling, but their customers were grateful. They were sure to have fuel for their fireplaces.

It is easy to guess what this little boy does for a living. The soot from the chimneys he cleans is all over him. He carries a shovel and a broom. He leaves black footprints in the snow!

Sidewalk sales

Walk down an early city street. How crowded it is! There are so many sights, smells, and sounds. The streets are not used only for traveling from place to place. Many of the people you see on the streets are earning their living. Do you see that man with a large box on his back? He is called a "trunk peddler." In the box are light items such as scissors, razors, pins, and needles. He hopes to sell these goods to people passing by. The man pulling the cart is called a "wagon peddler." He sells bulkier goods, such as fabrics, laces, hats, shoes, and inexpensive clocks.

Where are all these wonderful smells coming from? Many people, called vendors or **mongers**, sell food and beverages to hungry and thirsty pedestrians. If you are hungry, you can wander over to the cheesemonger or soupmonger. They are easy to locate because they are always shouting. Listen. "Buy your cheese here! Cheese! Cheese for sale!"

Going about their business

Mongers also sell coal, clothes, clocks, and almost anything else that they can carry or cart. If you run out of anything, it is easy to step into the street and check to see if a monger is selling the article you need. More often than not, he is!

The streets are full of young children. Not all of them are playing. Some of them are working. Look to the corner of the street. The newsboy is selling his papers. Look to the other corner. The shoeshine boy has set up his stand and is ready to polish any of the dirty boots that stop in front of him. There are some boys selling kindling wood. Look high up to the roofs of the houses. The young sweeps are cleaning the soot from the chimneys. Chimney sweeps were always small. They had to fit into the chimneys. After their work was done, they were filthy. All of these children who work on the street must make enough money to buy food and pay for shelter.

Street entertainers

People in the city often had to work hard and live without luxuries. On the city streets, however, they found pleasures that were more important than riches. They found other people. This trumpet player earns his living playing tunes. He brings the whole neighborhood together in happiness.

44

There were many ways to earn a living in the city. On the city streets, a good entertainer could always find an audience. This organ grinder makes little cardboard people dance when he turns the handle. A girl helps the organ grinder by carrying his money dish. People drop pennies into it to pay for the show.

Do you believe a bird could pick the cards that would tell your fortune? Mrs. Burns earns five cents every time her birds perform their trick.

Mr. Daniels is ready to set up his hurdy gurdy. His monkey is dressed for the show. Mr. Daniels plays the organ, and the monkey dances.

This is the kitchen in a city home owned by wealthy people. The servants are preparing food for a party. They seem to be having a bit of a party while they work! The servants made the best of their life downstairs. Their employers did not seem to have nearly as much fun upstairs!

Marie-Claire has just arrived after traveling from Paris. She is given a job before she has a chance to collect her trunks. Young girls were able to find work as domestic servants.

It wasn't very glamorous to work as a housemaid, but Marie-Claire enjoys her work! She is happy to have a job. She came to this country because she could not find work in Paris.

Servants in a city home

My name is Marie-Claire. I am sixteen years old and was born in Paris, France. Paris is an old and beautiful city but there was no work there for a young and ambitious girl like me. My family could no longer afford to take care of me. I heard of the small growing cities in the New World. I decided it would be best for me to go to find work there. I bid my parents adieu.

Marie-Claire becomes a maid

When I left the ship in the harbor of this city, I did not have to wait ten minutes before I had a job! There were ten or fifteen women at the port waiting for my ship. They are employed as housekeepers in some of the wealthy city homes. They go to the harbor to look for girls who want work. A woman named Bonnie spoke to me. I had learned a little English in France, so I could understand when she asked me if I wanted a job as a **domestic** servant. Mais oui! What a fine job, to do chores in a lovely house! And I will have a place to stay. The servants' quarters are attached to the main house. When I left my country I thought I might be a **governess**, but a house servant is a fine job.

"It's hard to get good help"

As we walked toward my new home, I asked Bonnie if there were so few girls looking for work that employers had to search the docks for helpers. She laughed. Bonnie said that even when there are few jobs for servants, it is still hard to get "good" help. Most servants think of themselves as temporary helpers. They want to work only for a short time. They want to save their money and then buy their own businesses. Also, Bonnie said, many girls are badly trained. They are sloppy in their work and disrespectful to the master and mistress. Bonnie told me that Mistress Katie wants an untrained girl. Bonnie will be in charge of teaching me to be a good servant. Would I be willing to work for Mistress Katie for a long time? Mais oui!

We reached the beautiful home. Bonnie told me that she is responsible for the housemaids and the kitchen maids. She is responsible for hiring and firing us, for making sure we keep the house clean. I promised her that I would work very hard to do my job well.

The butler and the cook

Bonnie introduced me to the butler. His name is Ferdinand. He is in charge of the dining room. He has been working here for several years. He came from Spain. Maybe we can speak together. Our native languages are similar.

Bonnie also introduced me to Karl, the cook. Karl is a big jolly fellow, but after smiling at me, he turned to one of the kitchen maids and gave her a sharp order. She immediately rushed into the **scullery** and started scrubbing the pots and pans.

Suddenly I heard a ring. I was startled but Bonnie told me that this is a special new system in the house. The bells are connected to wires that go up and down the walls and across the floors to the rooms where the mistress and master live. The mistress pulls the correct string for the servant she wants. Each servant's bell has its own sound. Bonnie says that this is her ring. "Come with me," she says. "Now you can meet the mistress." I hope that they will like me here. I will work hard and learn to be a good servant. Wish me bonne chance!

Jenny has a bad cold. She does not feel well enough to work, but she tries to clean the house anyway. She checks the time. She still has a long day's work ahead.

Mark has his own little sleigh, pony, and puppy. Frank, the footman, takes him out for sleigh rides when he is not busy working for Mark's father. Having a footman was like having a friend! A footman was a servant who answered the door and took care of his employer's traveling arrangements.

Charles spends most of his time with his nanny. Miss Stobbs is like a nurse, mother, teacher, and friend — all in one! It is Charles' bedtime, and Nanny is going to tuck him in.

Marie-Claire's new friends

Marie-Claire has settled into her new job as a housemaid. Even though it is hard work, she enjoys the chance to meet people from different countries. Many of the servants in Mistress Katie's house are immigrants. They all have interesting stories to tell.

Hans is an **indentured** servant. This means that he wished to leave the Netherlands but had no money to pay for his passage across the sea. Hans agreed to let the ship's captain sell his services as kitchen help when he arrived in this country. Hans has been working for Mistress Katie for seven years but he has not received any wages. The money for his work was paid to the ship's captain. Hans receives free room and board in return for his services. In one more year, Hans' period of indenture will be over. He is looking forward to working on a farm. He will move from the city. Hans hopes to have his own farm some day.

These girls have been hired to clean this town-house before the new owners move in. This is not a wealthy neighborhood, but children were sometimes hired to do odd jobs.

Stephen is looking for work. He knocks on the doors of homes owned by rich people to see if there are any jobs. The maid tells him that there may be some wood he can chop.

The footman

Frank is the house **footman**. He helps his employers in and out of their coach. He also has the chore of running in front of the coach when the master or mistress is driving through the city. He must clear traffic from the path of the coach. Frank wears bright colors and shiny buckles, which show people how important his employers are. Frank's job can be dangerous. He tripped in front of the carriage one day and was trampled by a horse. Fortunately, he was only slightly injured.

The nanny

Marie-Claire often misses her mother who is so far across the sea. Luckily, she has Joan to turn to for comfort. Joan is the nanny to the children in the family. She has been with the family for many years, teaching and caring for the children. She does not mind sharing a little of her motherly warmth with Marie-Claire. Over the years, Joan has become a dear companion to Mistress Katie. She is treated as one of the family. At Christmas and New Year's, she receives handsome presents from the family.

Joan and some of the other loyal servants are sometimes given extra pocket money. Leftover candles and other useful scraps are also given to servants. Sometimes, even hand-me-down clothes are given to Mistress Katie's favorite maids.

Changing roles

Marie-Claire began her job just as the relationship between servants and employers was starting to change. Servants were beginning to feel unhappy in their positions. They did not like being at the "beck and call" of others. More and more servants left the domestic service and worked at the factories. They felt that working in the "sweatshops" was better than waiting on other people.

Marie-Claire could not understand this attitude. She was happy to be working in a fine home for a good employer. She felt lucky to be employed in this exciting and growing city!

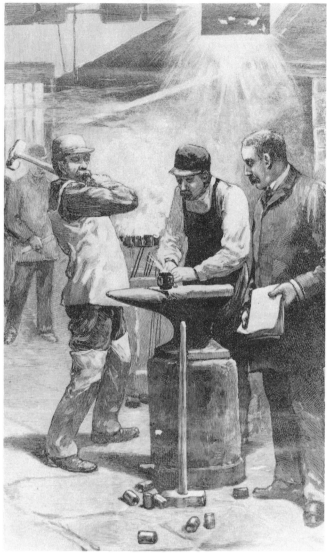

These men work at the government mint. They are destroying the molds that were used to make coins. The molds are worn out. The coins were made of precious metals, such as silver.

What are these men cooking up? They are counterfeiters. They are pouring cheap metal into molds. They will coat the metal with a thin layer of silver to make the coins look real.

Banking and business

In the early days people did not have the system of **currency** we have today. They did not have dollar bills or quarters. Some people simply traded something they owned for something they wanted to buy. This is called **bartering**.

For many years there were no banks. People kept their wealth in the form of gold or silver. They also used English **coinage**. Coins were **minted** by the government. They were made with silver. The early coins were easy to counterfeit. People made fake coins by coating cheap metal with silver. Even experts found it hard to tell the difference between counterfeit coins and coins minted by the government.

Confusing currency

The first banks were privately owned. There were no banking laws for the owners to follow. Each bank issued its own kind of bank note. Bank notes were used as money. There were so many kinds of bank notes that people were confused about money. If store owners did not recognize bank notes, they would not accept them as money. Today, everyone in the country uses the same notes and coins according to laws passed by the government.

Saving and lending

People kept their savings in banks. Banks paid people **interest** on their money. Interest kept customers interested in storing their money at banks! Banks then lent money to people who needed it to start their businesses. When their businesses began to make money, they paid off their bank loans. They paid banks interest on the money they borrowed.

Buying a share of a company

Some people invested their money. They bought percentages of a company. These percentages were called **shares.** As the company made money, shareholders received their share of the company's profits. People who made wise investments could make a great deal of money if their companies were successful. What happened to shareholders when a company failed? Mr. O'Connor will tell you.

Mr. O'Connor loses his shirt

*My name is O'Connor. At least, it used to be. Now my name is mud. I was brought up by hard-working parents, but I wanted to make a great deal of money right away. I decided to gamble. I did not gamble with cards. I did not gamble on the horses. I was attracted to the stock market. You see, in this country each company sells part of itself. That is, it offers a certain number of shares. Anyone can buy a share and own a small percentage of the company. The company uses your money, or **stocks,** to run its business. If the company makes money, you receive money because you have invested in the company. You are helping it to grow. If you buy a large number of shares in a company and it does well, you receive plenty of money in return.*

What could be more dependable than the gaslight company? There had been gaslights along our street for as long as I could remember. Well, I thought, this company is sure to have a bright future! Silly fool. I sank all my money into shares in the gas company. Then I made promises of great riches to my sweetheart. We had an expensive wedding, and I settled down to wait for the profits to roll in.

"We are ruined!" Mr. O'Connor has just read in the newspaper that the gaslight company has gone bankrupt. He had used all his savings to buy shares in the company. He is bankrupt too.

From riches to rags

Sometimes companies don't do so well. Now, if the gas company had started to slow down a bit, I wouldn't have minded. But it went bankrupt. It ran out of money. Electricity! Who would have believed that anything so incredible would have been invented? All my shares are worthless now. I have no money. We are ruined. Now I know better. I will leave the stock market to those with more brains and luck than I have. I will no longer look for quick money. I am going out tomorrow to get a real job. I hope the city will give me another chance. I think it will.

What a great idea!

Have you ever imagined inventing something? Inventors with imagination, determination, and plenty of luck could become rich and famous. Many of the gadgets we depend on surprised the early city residents when they first appeared in the stores.

Something as simple as a jar with a screw top was exciting! Before these jars were invented, people had to store food in crocks made of clay. Many other little kitchen tools were also invented. Peeling, paring, coring, and slicing fruit and vegetables became much easier. The fruit and vegetables were stored in the new jars.

The rat race

Both city and country people were plagued by rats and mice. Homes and buildings were never quiet at night. You could hear these pests scurrying around in search of food. Many people kept cats in a desperate attempt to control the population of rats and mice, but no Tom or Tabby was hungry enough to eat them all! People set to work to invent traps for the rodents. Soon a bewildering variety of spring and hinge traps were selling in the stores. It was difficult to know which trap could catch a mouse and which would simply snap at your fingers.

All sewn up!

The inventor of the first pair of scissors snipped his way to success. Everyone wanted to own a pair. Cutting with scissors was so much easier than cutting with a knife. Scissors made the work of tailors and seamstresses faster and simpler, but stitching by hand was still tiresome. The invention of the sewing machine took care of that problem. Some people attached fans and music boxes to the machines. On hot summer days they could keep cool and listen to music while they sewed.

Hitting the nail on the head!

Every time people wanted to build with wood, they had to make a trip to the blacksmith's shop. They waited while the blacksmith forged nails for them, one by one. Then someone invented molds for liquid metal. Nails could be made quickly in factories. Carpenters could dash to the hardware store and pick up a box full of neatly formed nails.

The birds made it look so easy! Inventors were able to make balloons that floated, but it took a long time to master wings. Still, people kept trying and failing. What a tangled mess!

The early sewing machines were powered with pedals. Seamstresses no longer had to sew by hand, but the work was hard on their legs!

This umbrella looked weird, but it worked!

A bouncing success

For a long time, going out in the rain meant coming home with soaked feet. There were no rubber boots. There were no rubber tires, rubber gloves, or rubber balls. There was no useful rubber. Rubber melted in the summer and cracked in the winter. Charles Goodyear discovered how to make rubber that was flexible in both hot and cold weather.

Umbrellas were invented late in the eighteenth century, but few people used them. Those who did walk in the rain with an umbrella were sure to be laughed at. People thought umbrellas looked ridiculous. Children would throw stones at them! Soon, people realized that umbrellas were more useful than funny. Before long it became fashionable to be seen carrying an umbrella down the street.

Lifesavers

Inventions made life easier. They also made life safer. Often it was impossible for a fire brigade to save a person trapped in a fire on the top floor of a building. Finally, a clever inventor designed a ladder tall enough for all kinds of rescues from fires.

The fire alarm was another life–saving invention. People heard the alarm and were able to escape from a burning building before the fire spread and blocked the exits. Water safety was also improved when someone invented life jackets and life preservers.

Flying too high

People were getting into trouble in the air. They were seeking glory by trying to invent flying machines. These machines were not safe at all. Most of them were strange and dangerous contraptions. The cost of trying to fly to fame was often too high.

Fires in tall buildings were disastrous when the fire escapes were blocked. Finally, someone invented a ladder that could be lengthened to save people trapped on the top floors.

Retail merchants proudly posted their store signs to attract customers. Many people came to open businesses in the city. Read the store signs. How many types of goods can you identify?

Children enjoy browsing in this store. Even if they cannot buy anything, they enjoy looking. The store owner sells dolls that he imports from many countries. He has the finest collection in the city.

Buying and selling

Why did towns grow into cities? As businesses got bigger, so did the trading centers. People came to the city to buy and sell goods. Merchants opened stores. They **imported** goods from other countries and bought products manufactured in this country. They bought these goods **wholesale**. Wholesale goods are bought in large quantities and at low prices by store owners. The store owners sell these goods in their **retail** stores. They charge more than they paid for the goods. The difference is the **profit**. Merchants earn their living by these profits.

Merchants in the early cities specialized in selling one kind of product. They sold linens or toys, clothing or stationery. When the first department store opened, it was exciting for the city's residents. They could not believe that under one roof they could buy almost anything! Many owners of early department stores made fortunes. Some customers, however, were still loyal to their favorite little stores. They liked the attention that the owners of small retail stores gave them. Today, department stores and smaller retail stores are open for business side by side.

Mr. Higgins loves books. He buys only the best for his shop. He makes enough money to keep his family comfortable. "Who needs a big, fancy shop?" he always tells his customers.

55

As one man unloads his garbage at the dump, others pick through the rubbish. They hunt for scraps of food, clothing, and anything else useful. Many people were so poor they had no other choice but to rummage through garbage.

Problems in the city

When a large number of people live together in a small area, problems usually occur. The early city was no exception. One of these problems was garbage. People threw away their leftovers instead of recycling them.

Uncollected garbage was piled on the sidewalks. There was no sanitation department to take it away. At one time pigs were the only form of garbage control. Other animals also roamed the streets, picking through garbage. Poultry, cows, stray horses, goats, and wild dogs were a common sight on city streets. All these animals, as well as the horses that pulled wagons and carriages, polluted the streets. In the summer the stench of animal refuse could be sickening.

Poverty and disease

People did not realize that many diseases were spread through waste and garbage. The settlers had no idea about germs. Only after thousands of people died in epidemics did people start to realize the importance of cleanliness. Cities started to clean their streets. Plans were made to dispose of garbage in a more efficient manner.

Life was unpleasant for many people in the early city. The city was filled with poor, unemployed, homeless people who had very little to eat. Sometimes these people had to hunt for scraps of food and clothing in the garbage dumps of the city.

Some children formed gangs. Often they did not have parents to look after them. Those with families were so poor that the children stole food. These children often got into trouble with the police.

Crime

Crime was a serious problem in the city. The early city could not protect its citizens as well as our cities do now. People could not summon police quickly in emergencies because there were no telephones. People hoped that if they were in danger, there would be a police officer close enough to hear their shouts for help.

To survive in the city, people needed money. People could not grow food on the sidewalks! They relied on the stores to supply them with food. Stores, naturally, demanded money for their goods. People who did not earn money could not rely on the government to help them survive, as they can now. Often poor people found themselves in desperate situations. They needed to find jobs, but sometimes there was no work. Some people felt that the only solution was to steal food, or money to buy food. Not only the poor committed crimes, however. Other city dwellers stole simply because they were greedy.

The punishment for a crime was prison. Many prisoners were crowded into one room with no beds. They were poorly fed. Some died of **consumption**. To many poor people, however, prison was no worse than life on the street. They felt they had no choice but to risk jail. The alternative might be starvation.

These farmers have brought their harvest into the city. They drive up and down the streets, selling fruit and vegetables. The farmers have had a long day and are eager to start on the journey home. Their customers are hurrying to buy food for their dinners. They are poor. They ask the farmers to lower their prices. The shoeshine boy is more interested in the tired horse than in the food.

Food

Would you like to shop for groceries at this market? Buyer beware! It has taken days for these farmers to transport their fruit and vegetables to this market in the city square. They sell their produce from the wagons. It was difficult to buy fresh food in the city. There was no quick method of transporting food from the country to the cities.

When customers come into this butcher shop to buy a cut of meat, the butcher cuts it then and there! The customers can choose the size and shape of meat that they want. The **carcasses** are hung on hooks. Customers can choose among beef, lamb, and pork. It was important to buy fresh meat. Meat spoiled quickly because the methods of freezing and preservation were not dependable.

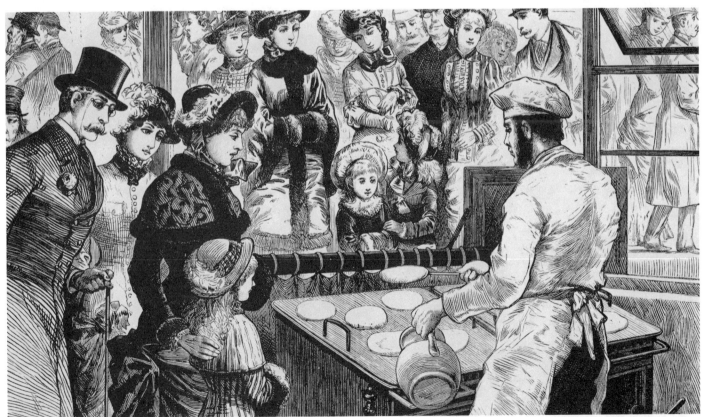

People crowd around the cook as he makes pancakes. They find his activity fascinating because this is the first fast-food restaurant in their city. The cook prepares the pancakes on a hot griddle at the front entrance of the restaurant. Many of the people in the crowd will want to sample the dishes that the restaurant offers.

The city offered special pleasures. Everyone could enjoy parks and open-air activities. Every Sunday there was a parade of coaches down the main street. People put on their Sunday best, went out in their shiny carriages, and visited friends and relatives.

Leisure hours

Pull up a chair and take a seat in a comfortable swing! The playground is always crowded with children and adults. People bring their hoops, skipping ropes, balls, and dolls. Some children are playing on a see-saw. Notice the way the children are dressed. Their outfits do not look like play clothes.

Miranda's cat is camera shy! Brian is trying to get a good shot, but the pet won't cooperate. Millie and Leo were returning from a tennis match when they came upon the scene.

Patricia was enjoying the zoo until this big bear got too close for comfort. City people flocked to the zoo on Sundays to enjoy the fresh air and see the interesting animals.

City parks often had ice rinks in the winter. Many people held skating parties. Some of the skaters liked to stand, and others liked to sit!

Eric and Sidney wait for their turn on this ride. The rides in the early amusement parks were not as fancy as those today, but they were just as much fun!

A refreshing change

Many young people poured into the cities from all over the country. The cities offered higher education, different kinds of jobs, more business opportunities, and an interesting way of life. The city was bursting with music, theater, art, and many social pleasures.

So, why are these city folks lying around in a country barn? Life in the city could often be hectic. City people soon discovered that taking a vacation in the country was one of the most enjoyable ways to spend a summer. City dwellers flocked to the countryside to discover the joys of farm life. After many weeks of milking cows, collecting eggs, and working in the fields, these folks were once again ready to take on the exciting challenges of city life.

Glossary

apprentice *a person who learns a trade by working for a skilled worker*

assembly line *a row of workers or machines which puts together a product*

bankrupt *not able to pay your debts*

barter *to trade one thing for another*

candidate *a person who competes for an office*

carcass *the body of a dead animal*

cesspool *a deep, covered pit for the drainage from toilets and sinks*

cholera *a serious disease of the digestive system*

client *a person who uses the services of a lawyer or other professional person*

cobblestone *a rounded stone used to pave streets*

consumption *an early word for "tuberculosis," a disease of the lungs*

copy boy *an office boy employed by a newspaper*

currency *the money that is used in a country*

deadline *the time when something must be finished*

deed *a written or printed legal agreement*

domestic *having to do with the home and family; domestic servants worked in the home*

editorial *an article in a newspaper or magazine stating an opinion of the editor or publisher*

eighteenth century *the years 1701 to 1800*

emigrate *to move from one country to another*

entrepreneur *a person who organizes and runs a business, taking risks and hoping to make a profit*

epidemic *the sudden spread of a disease among many people*

gristmill *a mill that grinds grain into flour*

immigrant *a person who moves into a country from another*

import *to bring in goods from another country*

interest *money that is paid for the use of a larger sum of money*

kiln *a furnace or oven for burning, baking, or drying bricks or pottery*

kindling *sticks or small pieces of wood used to start a fire*

landmark *a familiar object which may serve as a guide to travelers*

mason *a person whose work is building with stone, bricks, or concrete*

mint *to make coins*

municipal *having to do with the business and government of a city or town*

pantomime *a play without words, in which the players use body movements to act out the story*

privy *an outdoor toilet*

produce (pro-doos) *fruit, vegetables, and other products grown on the farm*

profession *an occupation that requires special education and training, such as law or medicine*

profit *the amount of money left after all the costs of a business have been paid*

refuse (ref-yoos) *anything thrown away as useless or worthless*

retail *the direct sale of goods to customers*

scullery *a room off a kitchen where vegetables are cleaned and pots and pans are washed*

seal *a design, used to show ownership, that is stamped on wax, paper, or other soft material*

services *electricity, roads, sewers, and other public needs that a town or city provides*

sewage (soo-ij) *the wastes that pass through sewers*

shanty *a roughly built hut or cabin*

share *one of the equal parts into which the ownership of a business is divided*

site *the position of a city, town, building, or other place*

squatter *a person who settles on land to which he or she has no right*

stock market *a place where the shares of a company are bought and sold*

sweatshop *a factory where people work for long hours and low wages under poor conditions*

tenement *an apartment house that is poorly built and usually overcrowded*

toll *a tax paid for the right to use something*

trolley *a bus run by electric current*

vendor *a person who sells goods, often outdoors*

ward *someone who is placed under the care and protection of another person*

wheelwright *a person who makes or fixes wheels*

wholesale *the sale of goods in large amounts to storekeepers*

Index

Acknowledgements

Library of Congress, Dover Archives, Colonial Williamsburg, Century Village, Lang, Upper Canada Village, Black Creek Pioneer Village, Metropolitan Toronto Library, Colborne Lodge, Toronto Historical Board, Gibson House, City of Toronto Archives, Bibliotheque National du Quebec, Harper's Weekly, Canadian Illustrated News, Public Archives of Canada, Notman Photographic Archives, Little Wide Awake, Frank Leslie's Illustrated Magazine, the Osborne Collection of Early Children's Books, Toronto Public Library, the Buffalo and Erie County Public Library Rare Book Department, Jamestown, Chatterbox, McCord Museum, Harper's Round Table Magazine, John P. Robarts Library

23456789 BP Printed in Canada 0987654